FAITH LIFTING PRAYERS

© Gregory Landsman 2019

Title: Faith Lifting Prayers, A celebration of humanity. Gregory Landsman

This edition published by Hill of Content Publishing in Australia
hillofcontentpublishing.com
office@hillofcontentpublishing.com
Correspondence: PO Box 24 East Melbourne 8002 Australia
Distribution: 77 Connaught Road Central Hong Kong

All rights reserved. No part of this publication may be reproduced by any mechanical, photographic or electronic process, in any form of a photographic recording; nor may it be stored in a retrieval system, transmitted, or otherwise be copied for public or private use — other than for "fair use" as brief quotations embodied in articles or reviews — without prior written permission of the publisher.

The prayers in this book represent the opinions of the author.
The moral rights of the author have been asserted.

Designed by Jo Hunt.

Paperback ISBN 978-0-648-28920-3
1st Edition, 2019

FAITH LIFTING PRAYERS

A Celebration of Humanity

GREGORY LANDSMAN

I dedicate this book to my wife.
For 29 years her love and spirit have inspired me.

I lost something along the way...

I wasn't born hating the way I was. But during my first year at school I became aware that the way I looked was not right. I was beaten, rejected and spat on. The pain of rejection literally tore at my soul.

I was a child of God; what right did anyone have to ridicule and abuse me for things that I could not change?

I was only six years old and desperate to understand why other children felt the need to do this and for the life of me I couldn't work it out. So, one afternoon I took all my clothes off, stood in front of the mirror and looked at myself from head to toe.

I stared hard until I could see the visible results of my six mixed bloodlines and what made me a physical misfit in other children's eyes.

All my differences seem to rise up and cut me into little pieces. For the first time I felt bitterness and anger in my heart. I hated everything that everyone else rejected, ridiculed and laughed at. Looking into my own eyes I saw that I hated myself.

In that awful moment I believed they were right and I was wrong. What was God thinking when he made me?

I was ugly and that became my truth.

But my story does not begin with the beatings and abuse, my choices, my addictions, or my career in the world of fashion and supermodels; it goes back to a Thursday afternoon when I took my first breath in the country of my parents.

Many people say that the country you are born in shapes your character. In my case it broke it down. I was born in South Africa, a beautiful place whose ugly Apartheid system ensured that I would be robbed from experiencing any form of self-acceptance. This system pumped out angry prejudice and gave me lessons that moulded my beliefs about which physical features gave me value and made me acceptable in the eyes of others. From as early as I can remember I knew that the colour of my skin, the texture of my hair and the width of my nose would determine my quality of life and my freedom.

At home my skin colour didn't matter, yet it defined everything beyond. I was learning the code of the black world and the white world and as a coloured boy, who was accepted by neither, I had to learn to fit in between.

In Johannesburg I was thrown into a schooling environment that was without doubt, the worst time of my life. I was constantly scared to death that my skin was the wrong colour, that my hair was too curly, my nose too broad and that I would be beaten because of my differences. Added to this was the terror of knowing that if I was beaten I could not defend myself against the bullies.

The boys at school saw my differences and punished me. I was like an alien who did not know how to talk like them, spit like them or kick dirt like them as they walked. I didn't know any of those things and more importantly, I did not want to know.

Being spat on and taunted, along with the fierce pleasure they got from torturing me with their insults, reminded me every day that I was a misfit. My differences were endless, and all I could do was try to survive when they descended on me in a group of five or more.

I tried to dodge the kicks, the fists and the vicious laughter that burst all around me. I was humiliated and beaten, my body bruised and dented, but beyond that I was terrified of letting my emotions out. My mind screamed, 'Do not let them see you cry.' I knew that if I shed one tear there would be no stopping the rest and I would never live it down. I had enough to live with; I didn't need any more names. To look strong, I battled the tears, pushing them down my throat even when I felt broken.

Every person's voice has a right to be heard. But I made a promise to myself to never let out any desperate sobs. Yet every day the urge to scream and cry out for help, to beg them to stop always rose in my mouth, but only for a moment. I would clench my jaw and keep my mouth shut. Not once did I ever cry out in front of them. I did not want them to think I was weak and so I never let them know that I was hurting.

And when the worst was over I would pick up my emotions along with any dignity I had left and walk home to my grandmother.

Back then I didn't know that being abused and spat on eats at the heart of a child's dignity and these kids fed on mine every day. I never really knew why they felt the need to do that.

At night I would sit on my bed in the dark and think, mostly about how to be stronger. I had to figure out how to be a better boy, but I did not know how to be anything other than what I was. Even then I knew that anything gentle or caring had nothing to do with being a man, and that I was not good enough in the eyes of so many in my life.

My sense of self suffered horribly and even today I can think of no deeper sadness than when we are asked to give up aspects of ourselves to prove our value. Nothing invalidates us more as children and adults than believing that we are not good enough. Nothing leaves us feeling more hopeless than when we know we cannot change aspects of ourselves that we believe are flawed. Nothing wrongs us more deeply than feeling judged, not only by others, but also by ourselves.

I suppose most of my lifelong insecurities were born in those days. Those children did the job of unbending my smile and breaking my self-belief. I was unaware at the time, but this is how I learnt to shame myself, to fill my body with hate and to know that cruelty lived in children.

But it was the self-hatred that came from feelings of shame, that I shoved so far down within my body that they unknowingly festered and rotted the root of goodness that makes us all human.

This stamped my life.

As I write this I feel the sadness of knowing that more often than not trying to look strong has nothing to do with strength, but everything to do with self-abuse. And as a child, rather than let my hurt, my tears or my rage out, I kept these emotions locked inside of my body until they broke me down.

My grandmother, or Ouma as I called her, was a deeply religious woman who encouraged me to talk to God. She would tell me, 'Only God knows.' But whatever he knew, he never shared with me. I did not understand his ways. I didn't know if he even existed. If he did, to me he was merciless.

Night after night we would kneel and pray together, 'Gentle Jesus meek and mild, look upon this little child,' but still every day I was beaten. My prayers got louder, yet nothing changed. I asked every night, 'Jesus where are you? Why don't you help me?' But I never heard from him. To me Jesus was deaf. All of my prayers, in the face of my fear and sadness, had no meaning. I was so angry at being left alone to deal with my torture that eventually I stopped praying.

My body constantly ached from the stones that were thrown at me and in a strange way being beaten every day affirmed that I was no good and deserved what happened to me. I began to believe that this was the reason that God had abandoned me.

My childhood footsteps became heavier as I carried my wrongness into the world. I hated myself and it felt like I was fighting a losing battle to be a boy. I must admit it took me many years and many experiences to recognise that if I wanted to be happy, I had to fight for my right to be myself, as trying to be someone else just never seemed to work.

My relationship with God did not re-emerge for many years. In my twenties I had a health scare that terrified me. When the doctor told me we would have to wait three weeks for the results, there was a part of me that wanted to pray for my health, to be strong, to live a healthful, happy life, but throughout my life my attempts to reach God had failed again and again. It was my own fear that my prayers would once again go unanswered that stopped me from praying.

I realised that my life was void of any spirituality. I could hear Ouma always telling me, 'God is good,' yet I had lived Godless for most of my life. I had to believe that whatever had brought me to this point had done so to heal all of the hurt and damaged aspects of myself.

I had not been on talking terms with God since my childhood, but when I got my medical results, I wanted to scream with relief. Instead I did something that surprised me, I prayed. I knelt down and prayed to a God I had wondered about for most of my life. 'Thank you, God. Thank you for giving me another chance.' For the first time my prayers were not the empty words that I muttered as a child. In that truthful moment I experienced the power of prayer that came not from empty words, but from my heart. This started healing my anger towards God.

More of Ouma's wise words came flooding back to me. She said that we all have different paths, but that all paths lead us back to God. There was a truth in her words I had never felt before.

Carrying the shame of my childhood into adulthood meant there were bits of me that I liked, but not enough for me to live a happy life. Ouma insisted that God had plans for me, yet for so long I had a difficult time accepting that.

Maybe it was easier for me to abandon my spirituality, because the day I made myself wrong I had made God wrong. I wanted to live a full life, to open myself to life and make sense of my confusion. I wanted to heal the aches and find the courage to face my sorrows and shame; as something inside was whispering that I had everything to create the life and love I knew I deserved, but to find peace with God, I had to find peace within myself.

My life lessons taught me that I could not outrun my insecurities and no matter what physical changes I made on the outside, nothing had changed on the inside. I was still a broken child walking around in an adult body.

The true irony of my life is that I have spent much of it in the fashion and beauty industry, in some of the most physically focused environments on the planet.

Yet it was through this polarised experience that I realised that I was no happier when I was accepted physically than when I wasn't.

At my lowest point, when I could run no further and had nowhere to turn, I turned inward, and for the first time faced my fear of having never been enough.

At different stages in my life I wouldn't have believed this, but I now know that the only reason I lacked belief in God as I grew up was because I lost belief in myself, my life and my ability to love. God didn't abandon me as a child, he had guided me to learn and understand beauty in real terms.

True beauty is more than a defined set of physical characteristics. It is faith lifting and expressed by each of us in the way we think, the way we feel, the way we live and the way we love.

It was through this journey that I came to know that there is beauty in every one of us, not just some of us.

Discovering this truth is a personal journey that we all make. And it is a lifelong one filled with moments of joy, sadness, tragedy and triumph.

For me spirituality is the freedom to love, honour and respect all aspects of who we are, all people and our lives. As regardless of our religious alignment, when we connect to the beauty within ourselves, we not only become spiritual beings, but beautiful beings.

If my years on this earth have taught me anything it is that it makes no difference where we come from, what we look like, where we live or what we do; as people, we are all worthy of celebrating our innate goodness as human beings and the vulnerability that comes with the physical body and the human spirit.

I called this book *Faith Lifting Prayers*, a celebration of humanity, because from my personal experience, when we combine faith with acceptance of our differences, the beauty of what makes us special and individual ignites naturally.

Knowing this inner truth helped turn my life around and I began to feel the goodness of God and the goodness of who I am.

Every prayer comes from my heart and is an affirmation that…

I believe in the equality of beauty
That no one is better than who we are
And in the same breath no one is less
In this truth lies our hope, our freedom
And our strength to live a good life

Gregory Landsman

Dear God

When it comes to finding the path to true beauty inside and out…

B   Bless me with **Balance** so that my heart and mind can work together and I can experience my beauty in a way that brings balance and harmony to my life and world

E   Bless me with **Enthusiasm** when I am feeling uninspired about myself and my life

A   Bless me with **Acceptance** so that I can accept myself with kindness and grace

U   Bless me with **Understanding** so that I can understand the truth of beauty

T   Bless me with **Trust** so that I can trust in who I am and what I represent in the world

Y   Bless me with your grace so I can rebuild faith in myself and feel the power of how **You** nourish my beauty and my life

Amen

BALANCE

Bless me with **Balance**
so that my heart and mind
can work together and I can
experience my beauty in a way
that brings balance and
harmony to my life and world

It is time to know the sumptuous beauty of my heart

To involve myself in the truth of it from the inside out

Let me set aside some quiet peaceful time to ponder its simple eternity

And to taste its life and love enhancing flavour

Amen

Dear God

When it comes to my beauty

I have pampered my skin

Conditioned my hair

Exercised my body

And monitored what I put in my mouth

But somewhere I forgot to condition my heart

And monitor my thoughts

I got caught up with my bone structure

And forgot that real beauty

Has more to do with the structure of my thoughts

Help me to remove all of my critical thinking

So I can remember this truth

And feel the peace that comes with it

Amen

Today I opened a magazine

And looked at the model images

I silently wished for their legs

Their flawless skin

Their silky hair

Page after page

I was smacked and baffled

By their physical beauty

Feelings bubbled up inside letting me know

That I could never live up to the ideal of beauty

I wrestled with these mixed feelings

'Oh how I wished I could!'

And with all the empty wishing

I began to feel a deep depression

I felt uneasy in my own skin

As questioning thoughts circulated

I couldn't understand

Why others were given so much

And in my mind I was given less

I felt a weariness

It filled my mind with self critical thoughts

And when I was tired of those feelings

I shut the magazine and closed my eyes

In the darkness I stumbled over many emotions

I listened closely to my yearnings and my fears

And only then could I hear what my heart
was trying to tell me

That 'BEAUTY' is only a word and I
give it meaning

With the way I live, love and accept myself

God let me feel the depth of this

So I can connect to the truth of it

And feel the eternal joy and freedom it brings

Amen

When it comes to my beauty

I have searched and searched

Through my continual struggle I am learning

That the beauty and love I search for outside myself

Are small aspects of what lie within

Give me the strength to go within

So that I will never go without

Let my beauty be shaped and nourished

By this inner truth

Amen

As I hopped onto the scale this morning

It tipped in a direction that made me feel bad

And then I thought…

'Today I will be good - no breakfast,
no lunch and no chocolate!'

Before I knew it, the calorie counting
war had begun

And that was all I could think on!

Give me the strength to eat in a balanced way

So that I know when I am full and when I
am hungry

To listen closely to my heart

So I can bring peace and harmony

Into my body and my life

And joyfully count my blessings

Not just my calories

Amen

Let me use each day to exercise joyously in any way I can

And do what feels good in my body

Give me the strength to run, walk, breathe, dance

Let me make the time to pray daily

To sing loudly

To meditate regularly

For it exercises my heart

Expresses my spirit

And allows me to remember

That there is nothing ugly about the human body

Only the love that I deny it

Amen

Let me love myself

Openly and honestly

Passionately and faithfully

So I can love others

In the same way

Amen

Dear God

Today I felt like a prisoner

Locked up by so many of my feelings

Let me transcend my inhibitions

And the insecurities that fertilise them

Let me make the bold journey upward and out

To free myself to find the joy and wisdom

That rests in the blessing of knowing eternal beauty

Amen

I was starving…

I was starving to feel desired and attractive. As a teenager I secretly longed for God to fix this brown skinny little body with big hair and protruding teeth that overwhelmed my face.

Every time I looked at myself I grew more certain that whoever handed out body parts had given me all of the ones that nobody wanted!

I felt like there was no place on this earth for a person with features like mine and believed that if I ever wanted to have a girlfriend I was going to have to look very different.

By the time I was fifteen it was evident that the most popular guys were always good at sport and used the sporting arena to show off their over-grown biceps, making mine look like little seedlings waiting to grow. In terms of body development, most boys seemed to have things pop up well before me and while they were sprouting big muscles, showing off their girlfriends and talking about the good sex they were having, I just felt grateful when a girl would look at me without laughing.

It was hurtful to believe that I was unattractive, but soul destroying to have it confirmed. I remember one particular day standing at the bus stop and seeing a group of five girls huddled together, giggling and laughing. For a brief moment I looked up at them and then looked away. As they giggled I thought that perhaps one of them was interested in me. Trying to project some level of attractiveness I cocked my head to the side, straightened myself up, slipped my hand in one pocket and puffed out my chest, much like a budgie in mating season. (I didn't have much of a chest to speak of, so the only thing that stuck out was my butt!)

Then one of the girls haughtily called out to me, 'Do you have a girl friend?' At that moment my heart thumped and immediately I thought my sexy attractive chest stance had worked. My voice quavered with anxiety. Faintly I replied, 'No,' and waited for a positive response that would spark the beginning of the romance I had so often dreamt of.

Suddenly she sniggered, sparking a chorus of menacing laughter, before telling me, 'We thought so, because you are so "*uuuugly*".' It only lasted a moment but nothing could shield my body from the word 'ugly', which seemed to echo in my mind, reverberate through my body and land like a dull thud in my heart. My stomach churned and I felt like something had been squashed down my throat. Their mocking laughter left me speechless and immobile. I stood like a voiceless dummy screaming internally with the pain of rejection and humiliation.

Giving in to the hurt, I panicked and I fought back the tears. I wanted to bury my face in the ground I stood on, partly for being dumb enough to think that they would have found me attractive and partly because I didn't know how to deal with the wild feelings that had consumed my body.

I looked around quickly to see if anyone else had witnessed my humiliation. I dropped my head in an attempt to conceal the emotions that were splayed all over my face. By the time the laughter subsided, a deep feeling of self-loathing and shame for not being able to respond or stand up for myself covered me like a blanket.

There were so many things I felt, and so many things I wanted to say, but instead I took refuge in the arrival of the bus, but lacked the courage to get on for fear of being ridiculed again. As they walked past me they smirked gleefully with complete satisfaction as if they had just stomped on a small meaningless insect.

The bus vanished and I was left standing alone. I sat down for a minute, slumped over, with my head buried in my hands. In that moment I felt the bruising weight of ugliness in my heart.

Until that time these thoughts had only lived in my head and somewhere in the back of my mind I had believed that someday my life could be different. But to have it shouted out by a stranger removed any trace of hope. I felt like their laughter reached into my heart and savagely tore chunks from it making room for ugliness to move in permanently. I stood up but couldn't walk without crying and as I cried I asked myself, 'Why me?'

I stomped home clenching my hands into fists that looked like tiny brown balls of anger, while my feet kicked anything in my path.

When I got home my dog Nicki was there to comfort me with a big bark. I picked her up and tears of humiliation ran down my face. I clung onto her tiny body and cried until I couldn't cry anymore. She licked my face with all its tears and I felt loved.

I never spoke about this incident because I knew that there was nothing anyone could do to remove the hurt I felt. That night was like so many others. I brushed my teeth then crawled into bed. In the dark stillness I closed my eyes and let my wild imagination run free. I would jump out of my own skin and envision having a muscle bound body, with blonde hair, blue eyes and sun-kissed skin - all the features I thought would give me freedom from the body that held me prisoner to my unhappiness.

The feelings of being different, separate and vulnerable can be devastating. We live in a world where differences are rarely accepted and where things that look different are often regarded as ugly. There is something about that little word 'ugly' that sends fear through our bodies when we believe it is associated with a physical characteristic we possess.

Ugliness is like a disease that can eat away at us. It grows within us from the time we look in the mirror and do not like what we see.

How painful it is to grow up in a world that appears to worship the physical body. How cruel we become, not only as children, but as adults, when we are not taught to accept and celebrate the differences in ourselves and other people.

On reflection, feelings of ugliness challenged my self belief and provided me with an opportunity to see myself and the world differently. As painful as they were, these feelings helped me to grow and broaden my perspective and redefine what made me a valuable human being.

Dear God

It has taken many years to understand

That if I believe I am ugly, I will know ugliness

If I believe my body is not perfect, I will know imperfection

If I believe I am beautiful, I will know beauty

It is in my power to choose what I believe

Guide my thoughts so I can choose carefully

Amen

ENTHUSIASM

Bless me with **Enthusiasm**
when I am feeling uninspired
about my self and my life

Dear God

Let me hop out of bed bountifully

Embrace opportunities with an open heart

So the essence of my beauty

Can emerge with grace and purpose

Realign my life with your spirit

The source of true and lasting fulfillment

Give me the wisdom to live in the now

Give me the clarity not to waste time worrying about tomorrow

Let me live each day as if it were my last

And as I go about doing what I need to do

Let me feel your spirit

So that you can guide me

And fill my heart with glorious goodness

That radiates your divine light wherever I go

Lighting up what is dark

Bringing joy where there is sadness

And hope where there is hopelessness

Amen

Dear God

It is time to live authentically

To dream boldly

And to know in the deepest part of my heart

That my life and who I am is not about limitations

But endless possibilities that allow me to rise up each morning

And meet this precious truth

Amen

Dear God

Do not let me take myself too seriously

Let me laugh fully

Let me laugh deliciously

Let me laugh openly with myself

So that I will always remember

That where there is joyful laughter

Beauty is close by

Amen

Dear God

Grant me the courage to face myself

And to give myself the permission to use my voice

For so many years

My inadequacy has bound my tongue

Inhibited my speech

And the things that I have wanted to say

Have been stuck in my throat

Words that needed to be heard

Lose their way on my tongue

So I swallow the words that are lost

And try to find new ones

I feel anxiety

As people try to complete my sentences

Wanting a sentence to slip through my lips

But somehow it clings to my teeth

My words are drowned out

By fear of being judged and laughed at

But I have a voice that needs to be heard

We all do

As my voice finds its way

From my heart to my lips

And to the ears that are listening

May it be nourished and shaped by self-acceptance

I give thanks for my ability to speak my truth

And even though it isn't as smooth as I would like it to be

It is my voice and I own it

My words belong to me

And I will no longer judge how they leave my mouth

But bless them because they belong to me

Thank you

Amen

Throughout my life there are so many times when I forgot my value

But each time I forgot, you sent me your earth angels

My friends and loved ones to help me remember

That I am beautiful, loved and lovable

Through their love, acceptance and respect I am constantly reminded

Of the power of kindness and its ability to help heal my life

Thank you for these angels

Amen

God please help me

To love openly

To love gently

To love truthfully

To love passionately

To love myself

Through my personal struggle

To continue to survive and grow

And through your grace and healing

Know that when I see how loveable I am

I see how beautiful I am

Amen

God I am scared

I no longer want to dance to the rhythm of life

In my moments of emptiness

Let me feel your joy

From my fingers to my toes

From my heart to my mind

So I can move through my life

With uninhibited passion

With strength and vulnerability

So I can celebrate the delicious beauty

I was born to know, live and dance

Amen

The sun keeps me healing

The wind helps my breathing

The butterflies keep me dreaming

Your presence gives me meaning

Your spirit keeps me believing

Amen

Faith lifting beauty ignited...

More than twenty years ago I travelled to India and it was on this trip that my belief in 'faith lifting beauty' was ignited.

Travel has always enriched my life in many ways, but travelling to India helped me break through and break down the negative beliefs that trapped me for a large part of my life.

The people, the chaos and its overwhelming poverty urged me to look beyond my own day-to-day existence and reassess my beliefs.

In the faces of its people I saw a courageous ability to embrace life, rather than hide from it and to show up every day no matter what pain was endured.

I felt an admiration for their strength and willingness to stand up again and again when life knocked them down. My struggle wasn't theirs, in fact it was nothing like theirs, but still I felt a connectedness as so many of us struggle to find our place in the world.

In India, every day is a test of survival and a test of faith. Witnessing poverty and death on the streets inspired contemplation, as I asked myself question after question in relation to how I had lived my life to date.

If I left the earth today would I believe I had lived a full life?

Had I shared enough of my skills with people?

Is what I did on a day-to-day basis something that contributed to the world being a better place?

I didn't have all the answers, but I handed them over to God, knowing that the answer to those questions would help me to seek the truth about what really makes up a good life.

On one particular day when I was out taking photographs in Madras, I noticed a small framed woman standing in the early morning light, untouched and unmoved by all around her, while her sari danced in the wind.

She stood with her back to the sun, glancing over one shoulder, revealing only one side of her face. To me she looked like she had been dropped from heaven, wrapped in a rainbow.

There was something oddly familiar about this scene. It reminded me of a fashion shoot where the breeze gently moved the models garment as she smiled, capturing that perfect photographic moment.

But this woman was no model and she was certainly in no glamorous location. In that moment she turned, and as if in slow motion, her whole image morphed.

To my dismay I saw that her face had two dramatically different sides that bore no resemblance to each other in any way. The left side was disfigured. A mound of purple sagging flesh hung over her cheek, forming a flesh-like drape that concealed any bone structure. Despite this, she turned towards me exuding an air of pride.

Our eyes locked, she smiled at me and then dropped her head to look at a child playing in the mud. With uncertainty in my voice I asked her if she would like her photo taken. Instantly her rich brown face cracked open with a smile that stretched from ear to ear. She nodded, then in a thunderous voice she called out to the entire village.

In response almost every man, woman and child gathered around to watch. I focused the camera and she gently touched her hair to ensure that it was in place. I admired her eagerness, remembering how I often had to beg friends and relatives to take happy snaps.

Unblinkingly she looked into the lens. Her gaze was so intense it asked me, 'What did this mean?' I knew what it was to be judged for how I looked as a teenager and as a child. Yet in my career in fashion I lived only in a world that focused exclusively on physical beauty. A world where the word 'beauty' was used to justify why some were considered privileged and superior; all because of their fleeting looks.

As I stood there I witnessed the raw truth of beauty. Staring silently at the sagging muscles on this woman's face I knew I was being challenged by a truth that deep down I had always known - that skin-deep beauty would never be enough.

As I lined up the shot, two tourists stopped and stared with morbid curiosity. The one said, 'My God, isn't nature cruel?' It is so easy to feel righteous judging what we think is ugly. It was clear that it isn't nature that is cruel, but rather our lack of compassion and acceptance of differences.

Undisturbed the woman smiled for the camera, showing me once again that I could not change or control someone else's reaction. As she stood with her head high she revealed that she had long ago risen up to meet her beauty and her truth. She was willing to embrace all of who she was and what life had given her, and she was not concerned about how others responded.

As I took her photograph I studied her face. Her appearance disturbed me as it brushed up against everything we are taught about what makes someone valuable. But when I looked into her eyes I felt deeply moved. She had a sense of calm acceptance and integrity that I had never seen on any model's face I had worked with, mine included. This woman was living in a cushion of self acceptance; a living example that the essence of our beauty lies not in our physical characteristics, but in the heart of our character.

Looking at her I was filled with a longing for something that I did not yet truly know and wondered how liberating it must be to have such a sense of peace within one's self; to leave behind the impossible ideals of physical perfection that so often stop us feeling good about ourselves. I could see so clearly the reality of beauty and in that moment a part of me vowed to help others do the same.

This woman held up beauty, hope, acceptance and courage amidst chaos, confusion, poverty and judgment. I could see that we are all taught to forget that beauty can shine through every face and that the power and true essence of beauty unfolds from the inside out.

When I had finished taking the photos, this wondrous woman placed both her hands together in the middle of her chest, lowered her head reverently, smiled and walked away.

I knew I could reject or accept the truth of this lesson, but witnessing the truth was too powerful to ignore. After she left I sat on the sidewalk and wrote what this teacher of true beauty had taught me:

'In life sometimes love presents itself in a form that is totally unexpected, Rise to the consciousness of the love, not the level of the form.'

Whenever I am tempted to judge someone I remind myself of this.

The day I left Puttaparthi this wonderful teacher of beauty was there to farewell me. She waved to the man who reminded the village that she was valuable enough to be photographed, and I waved good-bye to the woman who taught me the power of gratitude.

Still today when I give too much thought to the way I look, I close my eyes and remember a woman who was proud and victorious in who she was and what she represented in the world, and I affirm silently that a face full of beauty is a heart full of love.

In remembering this we are all free.

ACCEPTANCE

Bless me with **Acceptance**
so that I can accept myself with
kindness and grace

God let me know my beauty

Face the challenges that come with it

Open my heart to feel it

Clear my mind to understand it

Give me the energy to walk it

Fill me with love to live it

Amen

I have struggled with conflicting parts of myself

Only you know that I have been running away from my insecurities

Hiding what I would like to change

And trying to do whatever I can

To keep up with the distorted images of beauty

I am exhausted

Help me to accept who I am and what cannot be changed

So that I can rest the parts of myself that are weary

Heal the parts that I have wounded

And awaken the most beautiful aspects of myself that have been asleep

Amen

When my heart feels broken

Let me understand that it is breaking open

So I can feel the hurt of my insecurities

The vulnerable discomfort that comes with them

To feel the path these feelings need to travel

So that I can let go, in order to grow

Loosen the emotional knots that bind me

Let me feel what I feel

So I can put the broken pieces together and heal

Amen

God, give me the courage

To face who I am

And what I am

So I can live fully in the present

Not wasting a day, a minute or a second

On wishing to be anything

Other than what I am

Give me the wisdom to understand

That promising, 'Tomorrow I can do better' is a waste of time

As tomorrow may never come

Let me know better today

Right here right now

As now is the only time

The perfect time

Allow me to accept this

So that I can know the fullness of inner peace

And through this feel your goodness

To guide me not to waste my time

But to celebrate, live, love, heal and laugh

Fully and gloriously

Amen

When it comes to my life and the way I live and love myself and others

Grant me the wisdom to know when to move on, instead of holding on

And at the end of each day

Give me the grace to say thank you, and celebrate all that is still in my life

And the courage to accept what has left

Amen

God I see with clarity that I am not on this earth for a long time

That I must not put off recognising my beauty until tomorrow

Until I lose that extra five kilos

Until I tighten and tone my legs

Until I change, change, change

Allow me to accept who I am, as I am today

With your grace, let me look in the mirror

And use my eyes to see the flowers, not the weeds

Amen

In the name of beauty

I have seriously considered plastic surgery on my nose

Nipping it and tucking it

Shaping it and moulding it

Hoping to experience the sweetness of a perfect nose

But then I felt an urge to go outside

I went for a walk

And looked around at nature

I took a deep breath

Kicked off my shoes

I felt the earth under my feet

I lay on the ground

And looked up into the sky

I filled my eyes with smiling clouds

Smelt the sweetness in the air

And in that brief moment of silence

I let go of the illusion of beauty

My heart clicked open

And I went inside to a place I don't visit very often

I felt at peace with a deep acceptance for the body I have

And the ways in which it allows me

To taste the goodness of life

I am part of this beautiful planet

I am beautiful

Guide me with your grace

To cherish this truth

Amen

Things can change in a day...

I would never have guessed that the sound of snipping scissors would draw me closer to the truth of who I really am.

It all happened when I decided that my hair needed a quick trim before a meeting. I was living in Zurich and my fiancé Michelle, who was visiting at the time, volunteered to cut it. 'How hard could it be to cut hair that short?' she said. Well I was feeling trusting, so I said, 'OK'.

This is undoubtedly one of the worst decisions I have ever made! Unfortunately her optimism did not match her skill and the result made the back of my head look like rats had been feasting on it. Michelle thought it looked fine, but then again it wasn't her head!

I needed to get it fixed professionally and as quickly as possible, so I went into my creative agency, and after they all laughed hysterically one of the hair artists went about fixing it.

Just when I thought my bad hair day was starting to improve, things suddenly went from bad to worse. Rocking away to the latest Prince album while simultaneously cutting hair with electric shears ensured something was destined to go drastically wrong and it did. As the stylist was cutting near the hairline around my forehead the shears jammed, pulling out a large chunk of hair from the roots. To my horror I now had a bleeding bald patch in the front and a chewed section at the back. Two bad haircuts in one day!

Panic rose in my belly. I felt like I had been pushed into the deep end of a pool and didn't know how to get out. Looking at the hairdresser's face as he tried to loosen the shears, I knew there was no solution other than to say good bye to my hair and embrace one of my greatest fears – being bald!

The stylist clipped the remainder of my hair and then prepared my head for the straight blade razor. Totally mortified, I couldn't speak. I ran my fingers through my hair for the last time. After a swift and painless descent the blade gathered momentum as it glided over my head, simultaneously shredding every last wisp of confidence I had about the way I looked.

My eyes glazed over with tears, so I closed them hoping I would open them and be free from this disaster. Little by little my hair dropped all around me, laying at my feet like a peace offering to a long history of swirling and straightening to manage my curls; blow-drying; bad hair cuts; endless hair tonic to keep it healthy; and the many years of managing my fear of inevitably going bald.

Looking back I had travelled a long and unhappy road with my hair. Growing up in South Africa no-one wanted curly hair so I did what most children of colour were taught to do from a very young age. Every night before bed I would comb my hair in the one direction and then sleep with a stocking on my head to keep it straight. Half way through the night I would wake up and swirl it in the opposite direction to ensure there were no curls or kinks in sight the following day.

Despite believing as a teenager that my hair was one of my only physical assets, I was often taunted by family members who told me, 'Play with your locks as they won't be there for long!'

In my former career as a model I worried about how I would work once my hair started thinning, all while knowing that no matter what anti-balding cream I used, the only thing that would eventually stop my hair falling was the ground!

That day in Zurich neither Mr Curly or Mr Straight survived and with that, the 'hair battle' finally ended.

I was as bald as a baby's bottom and a crying baby at that. I had never seen so much naked flesh in all my life! In my mind I looked like a big brown chocolate derriere with a face drawn on it, decorated by the only hair left on my head - my eyebrows.

I walked out of the agency sporting a bald Buddhist monk look. Jabbering all the way home, with the wind skimming my scalp, I kept telling myself that it wasn't so bad.

I spent the rest of the day in shock, constantly asking Michelle if it looked ok, while checking my reflection in every window to catch a glimpse of my new 'hair' (or lack of), and getting a fright every time I did!

But the pain didn't end there. That night as chance would have it, Michelle had arranged to go to the movies with friends to see *Dying Young*. I didn't know the film was about a man with leukaemia who loses all his hair while undergoing chemotherapy, and having fallen in love with his nurse, decides to end his treatment so his hair can grow back.

As we filed out of the cinema Michelle continued to sob over the movie. Feeling self-conscious about my freshly shaved 'do' it gradually became obvious that everyone's eyes were looking sympathetically at my head, which was three shades lighter than my face, and assuming that I was also in the middle of cancer treatment!

What a day!

When I finally got home I went to the mirror and held my bald head with both hands, the way a mother holds a newborn. After a long, hard look I cried for the years that I had shamed myself and made so many aspects of myself wrong.

I had allowed past memories and self-imposed negative beliefs to overshadow my present life and I was finally ready to liberate myself from the beliefs that had held me back.

I closed my eyes, my thoughts silenced and I felt something inside my heart soothe me. It was a feeling that let me know that self belief lies sleeping in all of us, but sometimes it takes an accident, a push, a nudge or in my case, a bad hair day to awaken it.

I felt blessed to have my health and a lot more besides and I was ready to take back what rightfully belonged to me, self acceptance.

When it comes to my hair

I have had good days and bad days

Through my lifetime…

I have curled it

Straightened it

Changed the color of it

Tried to soften it

Cut it

Shaved it

Plucked it from places where there was too much of it

Longed to have less of it

Cried as I was losing it

Wouldn't go swimming because of it

Wished I had more of it

Poured hot wax over it

Felt distressed when my ears were growing it

And refused to lie naked because of it

The battle with my hair is one that I started long ago

God let me make peace with my hair and all the places that it grows

So I can accept it, learn from it and gloriously surrender to the simple truth

That there are certain things in life I cannot control

Let me celebrate the humbling lessons of hair

Amen

UNDERSTANDING

Bless me with **Understanding**

so that I can understand

the truth of beauty

When I take my clothes off and run into the ocean

Let me feel the rush of beauty

Let the waves wash away my judgements

Let the wind brush away my insecurities

Let the salt bathe the wounds that they created

Let my feet sink deeply into the shifting sand

So I am not easily overturned by my fears

Let me swim freely into the depth of my beauty

And float effortlessly in the abundance of its goodness

Amen

God help me to celebrate my goodness

To empty my inner world of chaos

So I can have the space to live in your world

Help me heal the pain from the past

And the situations that enabled it

The past is the past

Yet I struggle to find reason or meaning

For the pain and sadness I have experienced

As I feel these emotional wounds

Keep my heart open

So that I can cry honestly

Allow every tear that I shed

To help me reach inwardly

To pour the hurtful feelings

Into the loving arms of forgiveness

Let each breath I take

Gather the painful memories

And gently carry them into the well of acceptance

So I can rest and revive

In the comfort and peace it offers

Let these feelings spread through my body like butter

So I can move forward

And run towards life

Awake and aware

In the full knowledge

That regardless of what happened in the past

I can illuminate what is dark

And put together what is fragmented

Knowing this is how I can honour and forgive myself

And the ones who have trespassed against me

Amen

Dear God

Let me know that good food equals good health

But to never underestimate the power of good thoughts

The power they have to create beautiful feelings

And a beautiful life

Amen

When it comes to beauty

My lessons keep coming daily

Served up like fresh ice cream

But never tasting that good!

Some days I feel weak and alone

On these days give me the inner knowing to realise

That I am guided by your love

And inspire me afresh to know

I am as young as my self-belief

As wise as my words

As old as my doubts

And as beautiful as the love I hold in my heart

Amen

God give me the understanding

That even though I am by myself

I am never alone

For you fill the empty spaces of my life

With acceptance, love, peace and happiness

Amen

Love is our healing...

It has been more than thirty years since my grandmother died in my arms, yet not a day goes by that I do not think of her with deep gratitude and love that still warms me from the inside out. Over the years I have experienced love in different ways, but the love of my grandmother showed me that love is our healing and our only hope for a joyful life. My grandmother healed so many of my hidden wounds through love in action. She taught me that a gift of love does not have to come in a box, it can be in a smile, a touch, a kind deed or a silent blessing.

As I write this I recall my immense sadness, on my return to Australia from working in Tokyo, at finding my Ouma very ill. Each day she looked frailer than the last and for a while I refused to accept that she would not make a healthy recovery. Doctors suspected she had lung cancer, but she would not allow any tests, as she believed she had lived a good life and didn't want to spend her remaining years in and out of hospital.

Every day that I spent with her I cherished. Yet there were so many questions that burdened my heart and mind. I wrestled with trying to understand how someone who had been so strong and dynamic was now so weak and fragile.

One morning I went to visit her and found her still in bed. This was unusual as by this time of the day she was being bathed by the visiting nurse, but the nurse could not make it this morning. As I sat next to Ouma on the bed I looked into her eyes and my mind drifted back to my earliest memories of her. I recalled moments of truthful loving, how her plump, tender arms used to form the most comfortable cradle for me to lie in. She would rock me from side to side, and had this wondrous way of laying kisses on my forehead in between verses of the songs she sang me.

Ouma looked after me as a child and every afternoon at five o'clock she would ritually bath me with the precision skill of a racing driver. The face cloth would weave in and around my ears and over my entire body ensuring nothing was missed. She would then gently wash the soles of my feet, giving them a quick tickle. When I hopped out of the bath she wrapped me snugly in a towel and we would laugh like best friends.

As I got older our friendship continued to grow, but sadly the joy I experienced at home with her did not extend into my school life. My third grade teacher used to beat me for any number of reasons that she would come up with on a daily basis. I had trouble reading without stuttering and every morning my grandmother would wake me at six o'clock and I would snuggle next to her in bed so she could help me practice my reading. Ouma assured me that I was a clever boy who just had a very bad teacher.

One particular day at school I was beaten repeatedly by my teacher. Firstly she hit my knuckles with the side of a ruler for not replying quickly enough to arithmetic times tables, and then I was given thirty cuts (lashings on the palms of my hands with a cane) for stuttering in front of the class as I read. The pain was so intense that each cut took my breath away. I tried to fight back the tears but couldn't.

I felt humiliated and hurt and ran all the way home to seek the safety and comfort of my grandmother's arms. My eyes ached as much as my hands, which were red, raw and swollen. Without saying a word, Ouma gently looked at my hands the way a person looks at an injured bird. She reassuringly ran her fingers through my hair and marched me back to school at such a racy pace that I struggled to keep up. Ouma was like a hurricane about to do some serious damage.

She flung the door open and stormed into the classroom, taking the teacher by surprise. Her small powerful hand lurched upward and grabbed the teacher's throat, pushing her against the black-board. The teacher, wide-eyed with fright, struggled to get away but Ouma's firm grip and big belly held her prisoner. In an authoritarian tone Ouma said, 'If you touch my grandson again I will personally break your neck.' Then Ouma walked towards the wall unit that housed all of the teacher's prize canes. In one fell swoop Ouma snapped them all effortlessly in half over her knee, much like you snap match sticks with two fingers. The children sat in silence, looking on with horrified fascination, as though an action movie was being played out in their own classroom. 'This is the last time you touch him!' Ouma shouted at a high pitch.

We walked home together, her arm affectionately resting on my shoulder. While Ouma talked about the stupid teacher, I cried a little and then we laughed. My grandmother had this wonderful knack of being able to untangle my anger and sadness just by making me laugh at her comical expressions. Through the laughter I always felt healed.

As I sat with her reflecting on these incidents, it was difficult to believe how much she had changed. Her big love-filled body now resembled an over blown balloon that had been deflated, she was a shadow of her former self. Her dark skin hung loosely off her bones and her crown of black hair was now thin and white. The only thing that hadn't changed was the warmth of her eyes and the love that they reflected.

As we sat on the bed I said to Ouma, 'Let me bath you.' She smiled and said that was okay, the nurse would be here tomorrow. I insisted and reluctantly she accepted. When we got to the bathroom I undressed her like she had undressed me as a child. Her frail limbs did not allow her to sit in the bath, so I put her in the shower. By this point she was too weak to stand, and nearly fell over, so I jumped into the shower fully clothed to break her fall and hold her up. I was drenched, but she was safe.

I took her out, wrapped her in a big towel and picked her up like a tired child. She put her head on my shoulder and said, 'In all my life I would never have thought I would live to see the day that you had to bath me.' For the first time my grandmother cried in my arms and I was able to support her in the way that she had supported me. We both wept. We had travelled a long journey together and overcome many obstacles, not only as grandmother and grandson, but as true friends who shared a mutual respect and acceptance of each other.

While we did not exchange many words on this day, our hearts seemed to have a language all their own, chatting like never before, about gratitude, friendship, life and love. Her eyes and her gentle touch revealed many emotions that wrapped themselves tightly around my heart. It was at this moment I learnt that when a person's heart is filled with love, no words are needed to convey it.

The day my Ouma died, her face had a veil of love over it. She gave me a wide smile that let my heart know how much she loved me. Then she reached for my hand and we formed a heavenly handshake as she murmured in a sweet, gentle voice, 'You are a good boy who will always be blessed.' Then she took a deep, long breath that lasted for an eternity. She seemed to savour it, much like the last drop of good wine. I saw the strength of her love in her eyes one last time, and as she closed them, soothing tears filled with life flowed ever so gently down her cheeks.

I took comfort from her painless death and felt a sense of gratitude for the blessing of having been loved by her. What I feared with her death was that my life would be empty. But I learnt that love did not end when Ouma died, it kept growing and growing. My grandmother left an imprint of the love she shared with me deep in my mind and heart. This inspired me to continually feel the presence of her love and her spirit, and through this her love lives on forever. Love continues to grow when we remember a person's goodness and through these memories we keep love alive. This is the power of love.

As you journey through life
May you always celebrate and remember your beauty
May this beauty always dance in the presence of your love
And may you always nurture the house
That enables you to do this…your heart

TRUST

Bless me with **Trust**

so that I can trust in

who I am and what

I represent in the world

Today I looked in the mirror

And shed a tear for what I used to look like

I know I am still the same person

But I feel as though I have lost my youth

When I search for the meaning in all of this

Gently and lovingly remind me

That I have not lost my youth, just my self-belief

When I look in the mirror give me the grace

To keep an open heart and kind mind

So that I can feel more, heal more, live more and love more

Of who I am, just as I am

Amen

Today is a new day

I am good, loving, dynamic and beautiful

Let me feel this truth and live it

Amen

I know when I look in the mirror I am a fault finder

I pray for another way of being

Help me to use my eyes to see beauty

My ears to hear it

My tongue to speak it

My hands to create and share it

And my feet to walk towards the truth of beauty

God give me the strength to do this

And to know that beauty isn't always about getting what I want

But making the most of what I have got

Thank you dear God for all that you have given me

Amen

God smile gently on my shortcomings and forgive them

So that I can be the beautiful being I am meant to be

Let me bravely embrace the aspects of myself I have rejected

Let me joyfully and honestly live and nourish the beauty I know I have

Amen

Dear God

Bless me for my forgetfulness

My confusion

My frustration

My anger

My insecurities

And my fears

May I always remember

That love and beauty are interlinked

And with one, I ultimately share the other

Keep my heart open

So I can continue to love myself and others

Amen

In life I have lost many things

And some things have been taken away

But for all that has been taken from me

When I talk to you there is an inner knowing

That no one can take away…

My beliefs

My smile

My soul

My dreams

My memories

My willingness to love

My ability to sing in the shower

My passion for life

My beauty as a human being

Amen

Dear God

There are many things in life
I do not understand

Racism, sexism, lookism, ageism

But for all the misunderstandings

Help me believe in the goodness and beauty of all people

And to know that as human beings

We are all meant to be different

Give me the wisdom to know and accept this simple truth

So I no longer hurt myself or others

For the simple things that make us human

Amen

God sometimes I feel like I spend so much energy

Trying to cajole and control everything

It feels like I am wrestling life to the ground

From my nose to my toes

Give me the grace to surrender to the flow

So I can go and grow where my heart takes me

Amen

Dear God

Today I saw the most beautiful sunrise

Seagulls flying effortlessly through the pink sky

As I walked I smelt the fragrance of flowers in bloom

And watched the bees that sat on them with peace and purpose

Looking down I smiled at the perfect blades of green grass

The tiny ants that crawled over them

And suddenly a feeling of nature's truth and simplicity washed over me

Everything has structure

Our animal kingdom

Our nature kingdom

The stars

The moon

The sun

The ocean

And it felt that all is as it is supposed to be

I could see beauty all around me

Everywhere, except within me

I had observed beauty, but forgotten to feel it

To recognise that I too have structure

I surrendered to this precious truth

And reminded myself

That God doesn't make mistakes

And He certainly doesn't make ugly

Grant me the grace to nurture and live this

When I look at myself and others

Amen

Spread your beauty wings and fly...

I met a woman recently who had a deep interest in butterflies. She went on to explain the basics to me... that they start off as caterpillars, eating their way through leaves. They then cocoon themselves and eventually turn into butterflies.

What I didn't know was that to turn from a caterpillar into a butterfly is a feat of nature, a process that takes an extraordinary struggle for the butterfly to break out of the cocoon. But that struggle has a purpose. It strengthens the butterfly's wings so that when it finally breaks free from the cocoon, it is able to fly. She explained to me that if nature had created an easier process for the butterfly its wings would never be strong enough and it would die.

Much like the butterfly, strengthening our own beauty wings is a personal journey that with all its challenges takes us closer to the truth of what makes us beautiful human beings. This can be confronting and often we look at situations and wonder why things have to be so difficult? Why are so many of us challenged in this area of our lives, never feeling as though we look how we would like to?

My own path through the world has shown me that for most of us there is a certain amount of struggle before we reach a point where we are strong enough to simply be free and fly as God intended us.

So on those days when you are feeling challenged, for something simple or more significant, try to keep in mind that you are strengthening your beauty wings and getting ready to fly.

Be BEAUTIFUL, Be Free...

YOU

Bless me with your grace

so I can rebuild faith in myself

and feel the power of how

You nourish my beauty and my life

As the sun rises

Let me start the day

With an intention to feel beautiful and happy

I know there will always be times

When I feel challenged by the world's concept of beauty

Times when I feel that deeply cherished thoughts

About what I believed made me valuable and beautiful

Must be left behind

Give me the strength and courage to do this

So that I can choose to believe in the truth of who I am

And find it in myself again

Allow me to understand that this is the time

To create a new vision of myself

Let this vision be borne from the wisdom

To know my beauty as a human being

Amen

Let my beauty miraculously unfold inside of me

Let it unfold outside of me and below me

Let it dance beside me and around me

So I can experience the momentum of it

The importance of it

And the eternal joy of it

Amen

God, I know we are all different

But in spite of who we are

Or what we do, look like or have

Give me the grace to know

That as human beings

We all want to love and be loved

And in knowing this

We are free from judgements

And the separation they bring

Amen

When it comes to my individuality

Let me remember

Not to tone it down

Tamper with it

Or hide it

Let me know it

And grow it on the deepest level

Let me stand proud

In the strength of it

And allow it to shine

Amen

Dear God

Let me live honestly

So I worry less about what others think of me

And focus on thinking positively about myself

So I can continue to dream, wonder and express

The very best of who I am

Amen

Dear God

Let me live through the clarity and the essence of my beauty

Tapping into the power and energy of it

Affirming as I go through my day

That I am also an extension of all the beauty that surrounds me

And that you created so effortlessly

Amen

God allow me to know the beauty that shines within me

Let it shine outwardly as I go about my day to day business

Allow me to feel the fullness of it

To taste the life enhancing sweetness it brings

So I can share it generously

Care for it kindly

And commit to it consciously

Knowing I can't be all things to all people

I can just be myself

Amen

Dear God

Let me grow gracefully

Let me age gratefully

Give me the strength

To do this beautifully

Amen

My prayer for you is that no matter where you find yourself or with whom you share your life, let love be your motivator and navigator to guide you to have the courage to love when you are fearful, to feel the strength of your love when you are weak and to believe that you are valuable enough to love and be loved when you are faced with the many challenges on your journey.

Gregory Landsman

Continuing the journey…

Listen to the Gregory Landsman podcast
STRESS FREE LIVING.
gregorylandsman.com

NOTES

www.ingramcontent.com/pod-product-compliance
Lightning Source LLC
Chambersburg PA
CBHW062059290426
44110CB00022B/2648